THE WHITE SHIP

**A LITTLE BOOK OF POEMS
SELECTED FROM THE
WORKS OF
DANTE GABRIEL ROSSETTI**

**BOSTON, MASS.
WILLIAM G. COLESWORTHY**
1896

Four Hundred Fifty Copies.
This is No. 265

The White Ship

W ATER, *for anguish of the solstice : — nay,*
But dip the vessel slowly,—nay, but lean
And hark how at its verge the wave sighs in
Reluctant. Hush! Beyond all depth away
The heat lies silent at the brink of day :
Now the hand trails upon the viol-string
That sobs, and the brown faces cease to sing,
Sad with the whole of pleasure. Whither stray
Her eyes now, from whose mouth the slim pipes creep
And leave it pouting, while the shadowed grass
Is cool against her naked side ? Let be : —
Say nothing now unto her lest she weep,
Nor name this ever. Be it as it was,—
Life touching lips with Immortality.

CONTENTS

	PAGE
THE WHITE SHIP	9
THE BLESSED DAMOZEL . .	21
EDEN BOWER	26
SISTER HELEN	33
CHIMES	42
SOOTHSAY	45
A LITTLE WHILE	48
LOVE'S NOCTURN	49
TROY TOWN	54
THE BURDEN OF NINEVEH . .	57
THE SONG OF THE BOWER . .	63
JENNY	65

CONTENTS

		PAGE
STRATTON WATER	. . . .	77
THE STREAM'S SECRET	. . .	83
THE CARD DEALER	. . .	91
MY SISTER'S SLEEP	. . .	93

THE WHITE SHIP

THE WHITE SHIP.

HENRY I. OF ENGLAND.
25TH NOVEMBER 1120.

B Y *none but me can the tale be told,*
 The butcher of Rouen, poor Berold.
(Lands are swayed by a King on a throne.)
'Twas a royal train put forth to sea,
Yet the tale can be told by none but me.
(The sea hath no King but God alone.)

King Henry held it as life's whole gain
That after his death his son should reign.

'Twas so in my youth I heard men say,
And my old age calls it back to-day.

King Henry of England's realm was he,
And Henry Duke of Normandy.

The times had changed when on either coast
"Clerkly Harry" was all his boast.

Of ruthless strokes full many an one
He had struck to crown himself and his son;
And his elder brother's eyes were gone.

And when to the chase his court would crowd,
The poor flung ploughshares on his road,
And shrieked: "Our cry is from King to God!"

9

THE WHITE SHIP

But all the chiefs of the English land
Had knelt and kissed the Prince's hand.

And next with his son he sailed to France
To claim the Norman allegiance:

And every baron in Normandy
Had taken the oath of fealty.

'Twas sworn and sealed, and the day had come
When the King and the Prince might journey home:

For Christmas cheer is to home hearts dear,
And Christmas now was drawing near.

Stout Fitz-Stephen came to the King,—
A pilot famous in seafaring;

And he held to the King, in all men's sight,
A mark of gold for his tribute's right.

" Liege Lord! my father guided the ship
From whose boat your father's foot did slip
When he caught the English soil in his grip,

" And cried: 'By this clasp I claim command
O'er every rood of English land!'

" He was borne to the realm you rule o'er now
In that ship with the archer carved at her prow:

" And thither I'll bear, an it be my due,
Your father's son and his grandson too.

" The famed White Ship is mine in the bay,
From Harfleur's harbour she sails to-day,

THE WHITE SHIP

" *With masts fair-pennoned as Norman spears*
And with fifty well-tried mariners."

Quoth the King : " *My ships are chosen each one,*
But I'll not say nay to Stephen's son.

" *My son and daughter and fellowship*
Shall cross the water in the White Ship."

The King set sail with the eve's south wind,
And soon he left that coast behind.

The Prince and all his, a princely show,
Remained in the good White Ship to go.

With noble knights and with ladies fair,
With courtiers and sailors gathered there,
Three hundred living souls we were :

And I Berold was the meanest hind
In all that train to the Prince assign'd.

The Prince was a lawless shameless youth ;
From his father's loins he sprang without ruth :

Eighteen years till then he had seen,
And the devil's dues in him were eighteen.

And now he cried : " *Bring wine from below ;*
Let the sailors revel ere yet they row :

" *Our speed shall o'ertake my father's flight*
Though we sail from the harbour at midnight."

The rowers made good cheer without check ;
The lords and ladies obeyed his beck ;
The night was light, and they danced on the deck.

THE WHITE SHIP

'But at midnight's stroke they cleared the bay,
And the White Ship furrowed the water-way.

The sails were set, and the oars kept tune
To the double flight of the ship and the moon:

Swifter and swifter the White Ship sped
Till she flew as the spirit flies from the dead:

As white as a lily glimmered she
Like a ship's fair ghost upon the sea.

And the Prince cried, " Friends, 'tis the hour to sing!
Is a songbird's course so swift on the wing?"

And under the winter stars' still throng,
From brown throats, white throats, merry and strong,
The knights and the ladies raised a song.

A song,—nay, a shriek that rent the sky,
That leaped o'er the deep!—the grievous cry
Of three hundred living that now must die.

An instant shriek that sprang to the shock
As the ship's keel felt the sunken rock.

'Tis said that afar—a shrill strange sigh—
The King's ships heard it and knew not why.

'Pale Fitz-Stephen stood by the helm
'Mid all those folk that the waves must whelm.

A great King's heir for the waves to whelm,
And the helpless pilot pale at the helm!

THE WHITE SHIP

The ship was eager and sucked athirst,
By the stealthy stab of the sharp reef pierc'd:

And like the moil round a sinking cup,
The waters against her crowded up.

A moment the pilot's senses spin,—
The next he snatched the Prince 'mid the din,
Cut the boat loose, and the youth leaped in.

A few friends leaped with him, standing near.
"Row! the sea's smooth and the night is clear!"

"What! none to be saved but these and I?"
"Row, row as you'd live! All here must die!"

Out of the churn of the choking ship,
Which the gulf grapples and the waves strip,
They struck with the strained oars' flash and dip.

'Twas then o'er the splitting bulwarks' brim
The Prince's sister screamed to him.

He gazed aloft, still rowing apace,
And through the whirled surf he knew her face.

To the toppling decks clave one and all
As a fly cleaves to a chamber-wall.

I Berold was clinging anear;
I prayed for myself and quaked with fear,
But I saw his eyes as he looked at her.

He knew her face and he heard her cry,
And he said, "Put back! she must not die!"

13

THE WHITE SHIP

And back with the current's force they reel
Like a leaf that's drawn to a water-wheel.

'Neath the ship's travail they scarce might float,
But he rose and stood in the rocking boat.

Low the poor ship leaned on the tide:
O'er the naked keel as she best might slide,
The sister toiled to the brother's side.

He reached an oar to her from below,
And stiffened his arms to clutch her so.

But now from the ship some spied the boat,
And "Saved!" was the cry from many a throat.

And down to the boat they leaped and fell:
It turned as a bucket turns in a well,
And nothing was there but the surge and swell.

The Prince that was and the King to come,
There in an instant gone to his doom,

Despite of all England's bended knee
And maugre the Norman fealty!

He was a Prince of lust and pride;
He showed no grace till the hour he died.

When he should be King, he oft would vow,
He'd yoke the peasant to his own plough.
O'er him the ships score their furrows now.

God only knows where his soul did wake,
But I saw him die for his sister's sake.

14

THE WHITE SHIP

By none but me can the tale be told,
The butcher of Rouen, poor Berold.
   (Lands are swayed by a King on a throne.)
'Twas a royal train put forth to sea,
Yet the tale can be told by none but me.
   (The sea hath no King but God alone.)

And now the end came o'er the waters' womb
Like the last great Day that's yet to come.

With prayers in vain and curses in vain,
The White Ship sundered on the mid-main:

And what were men and what was a ship
Were toys and splinters in the sea's grip.

I Berold was down in the sea;
And passing strange though the thing may be,
Of dreams then known I remember me.

Blithe is the shout on Harfleur's strand
When morning lights the sails to land:

And blithe is Honfleur's echoing gloam
When mothers call the children home:

And high do the bells of Rouen beat
When the Body of Christ goes down the street.

These things and the like were heard and shown
In a moment's trance 'neath the sea alone;

And when I rose, 'twas the sea did seem,
And not these things, to be all a dream.

15

THE WHITE SHIP

The ship was gone and the crowd was gone,
And the deep shuddered and the moon shone,

And in a strait grasp my arms did span
The mainyard rent from the mast where it ran ;
And on it with me was another man.

Where lands were none 'neath the dim sea-sky,
We told our names, that man and I.

" O I am Godefroy de l'Aigle hight,
And son I am to a belted knight."

" And I am Berold the butcher's son
Who slays the beasts in Rouen town."

Then cried we upon God's name, as we
Did drift on the bitter winter sea.

But lo ! a third man rose o'er the wave,
And we said, " Thank God ! us three may He save !"

He clutched to the yard with panting stare,
And we looked and knew Fitz-Stephen there.

He clung, and " What of the Prince ?" quoth he.
" Lost, lost !" we cried. He cried, " Woe on me !"
And loosed his hold and sank through the sea.

And soul with soul again in that space
We two were together face to face :

And each knew each, as the moments sped,
Less for one living than for one dead :

THE WHITE SHIP

And every still star overhead
Seemed an eye that knew we were but dead.

And the hours passed; till the noble's son
Sighed, " God be thy help! my strength's foredone!

" O farewell, friend, for I can no more!"
" Christ take thee!" I moaned; and his life was o'er.

Three hundred souls were all lost but one,
And I drifted over the sea alone.

At last the morning rose on the sea
Like an angel's wing that beat tow'rds me.

Sore numbed I was in my sheepskin coat;
Half dead I hung, and might nothing note,
Till I woke sun-warmed in a fisher-boat.

The sun was high o'er the eastern brim
As I praised God and gave thanks to Him.

That day I told my tale to a priest,
Who charged me, till the shrift were releas'd,
That I should keep it in mine own breast.

And with the priest I thence did fare
To King Henry's court at Winchester.

We spoke with the King's high chamberlain,
And he wept and mourned again and again,
As if his own son had been slain:

And round us ever there crowded fast
Great men with faces all aghast:

THE WHITE SHIP

And who so bold that might tell the thing
Which now they knew to their lord the King?
Much woe I learnt in their communing.

The King had watched with a heart sore stirred
For two whole days, and this was the third:

And still to all his court would he say,
" What keeps my son so long away?"

And they said: " The ports lie far and wide
That skirt the swell of the English tide;

"And England's cliffs are not more white
Than her women are, and scarce so light
Her skies as their eyes are blue and bright;

"And in some port that he reached from France
The Prince has lingered for his pleasaùnce."

But once the King asked: " What distant cry
Was that we heard 'twixt the sea and sky?"

And one said: " With suchlike shouts, pardie!
Do the fishers fling their nets at sea."

And one: " Who knows not the shrieking quest
When the sea-mew misses its young from the nest?"

'Twas thus till now they had soothed his dread,
Albeit they knew not what they said:

But who should speak to-day of the thing
That all knew there except the King?

18

THE WHITE SHIP

Then pondering much they found a way,
And met round the King's high seat that day :

And the King sat with a heart sore stirred,
And seldom he spoke and seldom heard.

'Twas then through the hall the King was 'ware
Of a little boy with golden hair,

As bright as the golden poppy is
That the beach breeds for the surf to kiss :

Yet pale his cheek as the thorn in Spring,
And his garb black like the raven's wing.

Nothing heard but his foot through the hall,
For now the lords were silent all.

And the King wondered, and said, " Alack !
Who sends me a fair boy dressed in black ?

" Why, sweet heart, do you pace through the hall
As though my court were a funeral ?"

Then lowly knelt the child at the dais,
And looked up weeping in the King's face.

" O wherefore black, O King, ye may say,
For white is the hue of death to-day.

" Your son and all his fellowship
Lie low in the sea with the White Ship."

King Henry fell as a man struck dead ;
And speechless still he stared from his bed
When to him next day my rede I read.

THE WHITE SHIP

There's many an hour must needs beguile
A King's high heart that he should smile,—

Full many a lordly hour, full fain
Of his realm's rule and pride of his reign:—

But this King never smiled again.

By none but me can the tale be told,
The butcher of Rouen, poor Berold.
  (Lands are swayed by a King on a throne.)
'Twas a royal train put forth to sea,
Yet the tale can be told by none but me.
  (The sea hath no King but God alone.)

THE BLESSED DAMOZEL.

THE *blessed damozel leaned out*
   From the gold bar of Heaven;
Her eyes were deeper than the depth
   Of waters stilled at even;
She had three lilies in her hand,
   And the stars in her hair were seven.

Her robe, ungirt from clasp to hem,
   No wrought flowers did adorn,
But a white rose of Mary's gift,
   For service meetly worn;
Her hair that lay along her back
   Was yellow like ripe corn.

Herseemed she scarce had been a day
   One of God's choristers;
The wonder was not yet quite gone
   From that still look of hers;
Albeit, to them she left, her day
   Had counted as ten years.

(To one, it is ten years of years.
   . . . *Yet now, and in this place,*
Surely she leaned o'er me — her hair
   Fell all about my face. . . .
Nothing: the autumn-fall of leaves.
   The whole year sets apace.)

It was the rampart of God's house
   That she was standing on;

THE BLESSED DAMOZEL

By God built over the sheer depth
The which is Space begun;
So high, that looking downward thence
She scarce could see the sun.

It lies in Heaven, across the flood
Of ether, as a bridge.
'Beneath, the tides of day and night
With flame and darkness ridge
The void, as low as where this earth
Spins like a fretful midge.

Around her, lovers, newly met
'Mid deathless love's acclaims,
Spoke evermore among themselves
Their heart-remembered names;
And the souls mounting up to God
Went by her like thin flames.

And still she bowed herself and stooped
Out of the circling charm;
Until her bosom must have made
The bar she leaned on warm,
And the lilies lay as if asleep
Along her bended arm.

From the fixed place of Heaven she saw
Time like a pulse shake fierce
Through all the worlds.   Her gaze still strove
Within the gulf to pierce
Its path; and now she spoke as when
The stars sang in their spheres.

The sun was gone now; the curled moon
Was like a little feather
Fluttering far down the gulf; and now
She spoke through the still weather.

THE BLESSED DAMOZEL

Her voice was like the voice the stars
  Had when they sang together.

(Ah sweet ! Even now, in that bird's song,
  Strove not her accents there,
Fain to be hearkened ? When those bells
  'Possessed the mid-day air,
Strove not her steps to reach my side
  Down all the echoing stair ?)

"I wish that he were come to me,
  For he will come," she said.
"Have I not prayed in Heaven ?— on earth,
  Lord, Lord, has he not pray'd ?
Are not two prayers a perfect strength ?
  And shall I feel afraid ?

"When round his head the aureole clings,
  And he is clothed in white,
I'll take his hand and go with him
  To the deep wells of light ;
As unto a stream we will step down,
  And bathe there in God's sight.

"We two will stand beside that shrine,
  Occult, withheld, untrod,
Whose lamps are stirred continually
  With prayer sent up to God ;
And see our old prayers, granted, melt
  Each like a little cloud.

"We two will lie i' the shadow of
  That living mystic tree
Within whose secret growth the Dove
  Is sometimes felt to be,
While every leaf that His plumes touch
  Saith His Name audibly.

THE BLESSED DAMOZEL

"*And I myself will teach to him,*
  I myself, lying so,
The songs I sing here; which his voice
  Shall pause in, hushed and slow,
And find some knowledge at each pause,
  Or some new thing to know."

(*Alas!   We two, we two, thou say'st!*
  Yea, one wast thou with me
That once of old.   But shall God lift
  To endless unity
The soul whose likeness with thy soul
  Was but its love for thee?)

"*We two,*" *she said,* "*will seek the groves*
  Where the lady Mary is,
With her five handmaidens, whose names
  Are five sweet symphonies,
Cecily, Gertrude, Magdalen,
  Margaret and Rosalys.

"*Circlewise sit they, with bound locks*
  And foreheads garlanded;
Into the fine cloth white like flame
  Weaving the golden thread,
To fashion the birth-robes for them
  Who are just born, being dead.

"*He shall fear, haply, and be dumb:*
  Then will I lay my cheek
To his, and tell about our love,
  Not once abashed or weak:
And the dear Mother will approve
  My pride, and let me speak.

"*Herself shall bring us, hand in hand,*
  To Him round whom all souls

24

THE BLESSED DAMOZEL

Kneel, the clear-ranged unnumbered heads
'Bowed with their aureoles :
And angels meeting us shall sing
To their citherns and citoles.

" There will I ask of Christ the Lord
Thus much for him and me : —
Only to live as once on earth
With Love, — only to be,
As then awhile, for ever now
Together, I and he."

She gazed and listened and then said,
Less sad of speech than mild, —
" All this is when he comes." She ceased.
The light thrilled towards her, fill'd
With angels in strong level flight.
Her eyes prayed, and she smil'd.

(I saw her smile.) But soon their path
Was vague in distant spheres :
And then she cast her arms along
The golden barriers,
And laid her face between her hands,
And wept. (I heard her tears.)

EDEN BOWER.

I<small>T</small> *was Lilith the wife of Adam:*
          (Sing Eden Bower!)
Not a drop of her blood was human,
But she was made like a soft sweet woman.

Lilith stood on the skirts of Eden;
          (Alas the hour!)
She was the first that thence was driven;
With her was hell and with Eve was heaven.

In the ear of the Snake said Lilith: —
          (Sing Eden Bower!)
" To thee I come when the rest is over;
A snake was I when thou wast my lover.

" I was the fairest snake in Eden:
          (Alas the hour!)
By the earth's will, new form and feature
Made me a wife for the earth's new creature.

" Take me thou as I come from Adam:
          (Sing Eden Bower!)
Once again shall my love subdue thee;
The past is past and I am come to thee.

" O but Adam was thrall to Lilith!
          (Alas the hour!)
All the threads of my hair are golden,
And there in a net his heart was holden.

EDEN BOWER

" *O and Lilith was queen of Adam!*
(Sing Eden Bower!)
All the day and the night together
My breath could shake his soul like a feather.

" *What great joys had Adam and Lilith!* —
(Alas the hour!)
Sweet close rings of the serpent's twining,
As heart in heart lay sighing and pining.

" *What bright babes had Lilith and Adam!* —
(Sing Eden Bower!)
Shapes that coiled in the woods and waters,
Glittering sons and radiant daughters.

" *O thou God, the Lord God of Eden!*
(Alas the hour!)
Say, was this fair body for no man,
That of Adam's flesh thou mak'st him a woman?

" *O thou Snake, the King-snake of Eden!*
(Sing Eden Bower!)
God's strong will our necks are under,
But thou and I may cleave it in sunder.

" *Help, sweet Snake, sweet lover of Lilith!*
(Alas the hour!)
And let God learn how I loved and hated
Man in the image of God created.

" *Help me once against Eve and Adam!*
(Sing Eden Bower!)
Help me once for this one endeavour,
And then my love shall be thine for ever!

" *Strong is God, the fell foe of Lilith:*
(Alas the hour!)
Nought in heaven or earth may affright Him;
But join thou with me and we will smite Him.

EDEN BOWER

"*Strong is God, the great God of Eden:*
(Sing Eden Bower!)
Over all He made He hath power;
But lend me thou thy shape for an hour!

"*Lend thy shape for the love of Lilith!*
(Alas the hour!)
Look, my mouth and my cheek are ruddy,
And thou art cold, and fire is my body.

"*Lend thy shape for the hate of Adam!*
(Sing Eden Bower!)
That he may wail my joy that forsook him,
And curse the day when the bride-sleep took him.

"*Lend thy shape for the shame of Eden!*
(Alas the hour!)
Is not the foe-God weak as the foeman
When love grows hate in the heart of a woman?

"*Wouldst thou know the heart's hope of Lilith?*
(Sing Eden Bower!)
Then bring thou close thine head till it glisten
Along my breast, and lip me and listen.

"*Am I sweet, O sweet Snake of Eden?*
(Alas the hour!)
Then ope thine ear to my warm mouth's cooing
And learn what deed remains for our doing.

"*Thou didst hear when God said to Adam:—*
(Sing Eden Bower!)
'*Of all this wealth I have made thee warden;*
Thou'rt free to eat of the trees of the garden:

"'*Only of one tree eat not in Eden;*
(Alas the hour!)
All save one I give to thy freewill,—
The Tree of the Knowledge of Good and Evil.'

EDEN BOWER

"O my love, come nearer to Lilith!
          (Sing Eden Bower!)
In thy sweet folds bind me and bend me,
&nd let me feel the shape thou shalt lend me!

"In thy shape I'll go back to Eden;
          (Alas the hour!)
In these coils that Tree will I grapple,
And stretch this crowned head forth by the apple.

"Lo, Eve bends to the breath of Lilith!
          (Sing Eden Bower!)
O how then shall my heart desire
All her blood as food to its fire!

"Lo, Eve bends to the words of Lilith! —
          (Alas the hour!)
'Nay, this Tree's fruit,—why should ye hate it,
Or Death be born the day that ye ate it?

"'Nay, but on that great day in Eden,
          (Sing Eden Bower!)
By the help that in this wise Tree is,
God knows well ye shall be as He is.'

"Then Eve shall eat and give unto Adam;
          (Alas the hour!)
And then they both shall know they are naked,
And their hearts ache as my heart hath ached.

"Ay, let them hide 'mid the trees of Eden,
          (Sing Eden Bower!)
As in the cool of the day in the garden
God shall walk without pity or pardon.

"Hear, thou Eve, the man's heart in Adam!
          (Alas the hour!)
Of his brave words hark to the bravest:—
'This the woman gave that thou gavest.'

EDEN BOWER

"Hear Eve speak, yea list to her, Lilith!
  (Sing Eden Bower!)
Feast thine heart with words that shall sate it —
' This the serpent gave and I ate it.'

" O proud Eve, cling close to thine Adam,
  (Alas the hour!)
Driven forth as the beasts of his naming
By the sword that for ever is flaming.

" Know, thy path is known unto Lilith!
  (Sing Eden Bower!)
While the blithe birds sang at thy wedding,
There her tears grew thorns for thy treading.

" O my love, thou Love-snake of Eden!
  (Alas the hour!)
O to-day and the day to come after!
Loose me, love, — give breath to my laughter.

" O bright Snake, the Death-worm of Adam!
  (Sing Eden Bower!)
Wreathe thy neck with my hair's bright tether,
And wear my gold and thy gold together!

" On that day on the skirts of Eden,
  (Alas the hour!)
In thy shape shall I glide back to thee,
And in my shape for an instant view thee.

" But when thou'rt thou and Lilith is Lilith,
  (Sing Eden Bower!)
In what bliss past hearing or seeing
Shall each one drink of the other's being!

" With cries of ' Eve!' and ' Eden!' and ' Adam!'
  (Alas the hour!)
How shall we mingle our love's caresses,
I in thy coils, and thou in my tresses!

EDEN BOWER

" *With those names, ye echoes of Eden,*
               (Sing Eden Bower!)
Fire shall cry from my heart that burneth,—
' Dust he is and to dust returneth!'

" *Yet to-day, thou master of Lilith,—*
               (Alas the hour!)
Wrap me round in the form I'll borrow
And let me tell thee of sweet to-morrow.

" *In the planted garden eastward in Eden,*
               (Sing Eden Bower!)
Where the river goes forth to water the garden,
The springs shall dry and the soil shall harden.

" *Yea, where the bride-sleep fell upon Adam,*
               (Alas the hour!)
None shall hear when the storm-wind whistles
Through roses choked among thorns and thistles.

" *Yea, beside the east-gate of Eden,*
               (Sing Eden Bower!)
Where God joined them and none might sever,
The sword turns this way and that for ever.

" *What of Adam cast out of Eden?*
               (Alas the hour!)
Lo! with care like a shadow shaken,
He tills the hard earth whence he was taken.

" *What of Eve too, cast out of Eden?*
               (Sing Eden Bower!)
Nay, but she, the bride of God's giving,
Must yet be mother of all men living.

" *Lo, God's grace, by the grace of Lilith!*
               (Alas the hour!)
To Eve's womb, from our sweet to-morrow,
God shall greatly multiply sorrow.

EDEN BOWER

"Fold me fast, O God-snake of Eden!
   (Sing Eden Bower!)
What more prize than love to impel thee?
Grip and lip my limbs as I tell thee!

"Lo! two babes for Eve and for Adam!
   (Alas the hour!)
Lo! sweet Snake, the travail and treasure, —
Two men-children born for their pleasure!

" The first is Cain and the second Abel:
   (Sing Eden Bower!)
The soul of one shall be made thy brother,
And thy tongue shall lap the blood of the other."
   (Alas the hour!)

SISTER HELEN.

"WHY *did you melt your waxen man,*
                    Sister Helen?
To-day is the third since you began."
" *The time was long, yet the time ran,*
                    Little brother."
                    (O Mother, Mary Mother,
Three days to-day, between Hell and Heaven!)

" *But if you have done your work aright,*
                    Sister Helen,
You'll let me play, for you said I might."
" *Be very still in your play to-night,*
                    Little Brother."
                    (O Mother, Mary Mother,
Third night, to-night, between Hell and Heaven!)

" *You said it must melt ere vesper-bell,*
                    Sister Helen;
If now it be molten, all is well."
" *Even so,—nay, peace! you cannot tell,*
                    Little brother."
                    (O Mother, Mary Mother,
O what is this, between Hell and Heaven?)

" *Oh the waxen knave was plump to-day,*
                    Sister Helen;
How like dead folk he has dropped away!"
" *Nay now, of the dead what can you say,*
                    Little brother?"
                    (O Mother, Mary Mother,
What of the dead, between Hell and Heaven?)

SISTER HELEN

"See, see, the sunken pile of wood,
                    Sister Helen,
Shines through the thinned wax red as blood!"
"Nay now, when looked you yet on blood,
                    Little brother?"
                    (O Mother, Mary Mother,
How pale she is, between Hell and Heaven!)

"Now close your eyes, for they're sick and sore,
                    Sister Helen,
And I'll play without the gallery door."
"Aye, let me rest,—I'll lie on the floor,
                    Little brother."
                    (O Mother, Mary Mother,
What rest to-night, between Hell and Heaven?)

"Here high up in the balcony,
                    Sister Helen,
The moon flies face to face with me."
"Aye, look and say whatever you see,
                    Little brother."
                    (O Mother, Mary Mother,
What sight to-night, between Hell and Heaven?)

"Outside it's merry in the wind's wake,
                    Sister Helen;
In the shaken trees the chill stars shake."
"Hush, heard you a horse-tread as you spake,
                    Little brother?"
                    (O Mother, Mary Mother,
What sound to-night, between Hell and Heaven?)

"I hear a horse-tread, and I see,
                    Sister Helen,
Three horsemen that ride terribly."
"Little brother, whence come the three,
                    Little brother?"
                    (O Mother, Mary Mother,
Whence should they come, between Hell and Heaven?)

34

SISTER HELEN

" *They come by the hill-verge from Boyne Bar,*
        Sister Helen,
And one draws nigh, but two are afar."
" *Look, look, do you know them who they are,*
        Little brother?"
        (O Mother, Mary Mother,
Who should they be, between Hell and Heaven?)

" *Oh, it's Keith of Eastholm rides so fast,*
        Sister Helen,
For I know the white mane on the blast."
" *The hour has come, has come at last,*
        Little brother!"
        (O Mother, Mary Mother,
Her hour at last, between Hell and Heaven!)

" *He has made a sign and called* " *Halloo!*
        Sister Helen,
And he says that he would speak with you."
" *Oh tell him I fear the frozen dew,*
        Little brother."
        (O Mother, Mary Mother,
Why laughs she thus, between Hell and Heaven?)

" *The wind is loud, but I hear him cry,*
        Sister Helen,
That Keith of Ewern's like to die."
" *And he and thou, and thou and I,*
        Little brother."
        (O Mother, Mary Mother,
And they and we, between Hell and Heaven!)

" *Three days ago, on his marriage-morn,*
        Sister Helen,
He sickened, and lies since then forlorn."
" *For bridegroom's side is the bride a thorn,*
        Little brother?"
        (O Mother, Mary Mother,
Cold bridal cheer, between Hell and Heaven!)

SISTER HELEN

" Three days and nights he has lain abed,
Sister Helen,
And he prays in torment to be dead."
" The thing may chance, if he have prayed,
Little brother !"
(O Mother, Mary Mother,
If he have prayed, between Hell and Heaven!)

" But he has not ceased to cry to-day,
Sister Helen,
That you should take your curse away."
" My prayer was heard, — he need but pray,
Little brother !"
(O Mother, Mary Mother,
Shall God not hear, between Hell and Heaven?)

" But he says, till you take back your ban,
Sister Helen,
His soul would pass, yet never can. "
" Nay then, shall I slay a living man,
Little brother ?"
(O Mother, Mary Mother,
A living soul, between Hell and Heaven!)

" But he calls for ever on your name,
Sister Helen,
And says that he melts before a flame."
" My heart for his pleasure fared the same,
Little brother."
(O Mother, Mary Mother,
Fire at the heart, between Hell and Heaven!)

"Here's Keith of Westholm riding fast,
Sister Helen,
For I know the white plume on the blast."
" The hour, the sweet hour I forecast,
Little brother !"
(O Mother, Mary Mother,
Is the hour sweet, between Hell and Heaven?)

36

SISTER HELEN

"*He stops to speak, and he stills his horse,*
                    Sister Helen;
But his words are drowned in the wind's course."
"*Nay hear, nay hear, you must hear perforce,*
                    Little brother!"
            (O Mother, Mary Mother,
What word now heard, between Hell and Heaven!)

"*Oh he says that Keith of Ewern's cry,*
                    Sister Helen,
Is ever to see you ere he die."
"*In all that his soul sees, there am I,*
                    Little brother!"
            (O Mother, Mary Mother,
The soul's one sight, between Hell and Heaven!)

"*He sends a ring and a broken coin,*
                    Sister Helen,
And bids you mind the banks of Boyne."
"*What else he broke will he ever join,*
                    Little brother?"
            (O Mother, Mary Mother,
No, never joined, between Hell and Heaven!)

"*He yields you these and craves full fain,*
                    Sister Helen,
You pardon him in his mortal pain."
"*What else he took will he give again,*
                    Little brother?"
            (O Mother, Mary Mother,
Not twice to give, between Hell and Heaven!)

"*He calls your name in an agony,*
                    Sister Helen,
That even dead Love must weep to see."
"*Hate, born of Love, is blind as he,*
                    Little brother!"
            (O Mother, Mary Mother,
Love turned to hate, between Hell and Heaven!)

37

SISTER HELEN

"*Oh it's Keith of Keith now that rides fast,*
            Sister Helen,
For I know the white hair on the blast."
"*The short short hour will soon be past,*
            Little brother!"
            (O Mother, Mary Mother,
Will soon be past, between Hell and Heaven!)

"*He looks at me and he tries to speak,*
            Sister Helen,
But oh! his voice is sad and weak!"
"*What here should the mighty Baron seek,*
            Little brother?"
            (O Mother, Mary Mother,
Is this the end, between Hell and Heaven?)

"*Oh his son still cries, if you forgive,*
            Sister Helen,
The body dies but the soul shall live."
"*Fire shall forgive me as I forgive,*
            Little brother!"
            (O Mother, Mary Mother,
As she forgives, between Hell and Heaven!)

"*Oh he prays you, as his heart would rive,*
            Sister Helen,
To save his dear son's soul alive."
"*Fire cannot slay it, it shall thrive,*
            Little brother!"
            (O Mother, Mary Mother,
Alas, alas, between Hell and Heaven!)

"*He cries to you, kneeling in the road,*
            Sister Helen,
To go with him for the love of God!"
"*The way is long to his son's abode,*
            Little brother."
            (O Mother, Mary Mother,
The way is long, between Hell and Heaven!)

38

SISTER HELEN

"*A lady's here, by a dark steed brought,*
            Sister Helen,
So darkly clad, I saw her not."
"*See her now or never see aught,*
            Little brother !"
            (O Mother, Mary Mother,
What more to see, between Hell and Heaven?)

"*Her hood falls back, and the moon shines fair,*
            Sister Helen,
On the Lady of Ewern's golden hair."
"*Blest hour of my power and her despair,*
            Little brother !"
            (O Mother, Mary Mother,
Hour blest and bann'd, between Hell and Heaven!)

"*Pale, pale her cheeks that in pride did glow,*
            Sister Helen,
'Neath the bridal-wreath three days ago."
"*One morn for pride and three days for woe,*
            Little brother !"
            (O Mother, Mary Mother,
Three days, three nights, between Hell and Heaven!)

"*Her clasped hands stretch from her bending head,*
            Sister Helen;
With the loud wind's wail her sobs are wed."
"*What wedding-strains hath her bridal-bed,*
            Little brother ?"
            (O Mother, Mary Mother,
What strain but death's, between Hell and Heaven?)

"*She may not speak, she sinks in a swoon,*
            Sister Helen,—
She lifts her lips and gasps on the moon."
"*Oh! might I but hear her soul's blithe tune,*
            Little brother !"
            (O Mother, Mary Mother,
Her woe's dumb cry, between Hell and Heaven!)

SISTER HELEN

"*They've caught her to Westholm's saddle-bow,*
        Sister Helen,
And her moonlit hair gleams white in its flow."
"*Let it turn whiter than winter snow,*
            Little brother!"
        (O Mother, Mary Mother,
Woe-withered gold, between Hell and Heaven!)

"*O Sister Helen, you heard the bell,*
        Sister Helen!
More loud than the vesper-chime it fell."
"*No vesper-chime, but a dying knell,*
            Little brother!"
        (O Mother, Mary Mother,
His dying knell, between Hell and Heaven!)

"*Alas! but I fear the heavy sound,*
        Sister Helen;
Is it in the sky or in the ground?"
"*Say, have they turned their horses round,*
            Little brother?"
        (O Mother, Mary Mother,
What would she more, between Hell and Heaven?)

"*They have raised the old man from his knee,*
        Sister Helen,
And they ride in silence hastily."
"*More fast the naked soul doth flee,*
            Little brother!"
        (O Mother, Mary Mother,
The naked soul, between Hell and Heaven!)

"*Flank to flank are the three steeds gone,*
        Sister Helen,
But the lady's dark steed goes alone."
"*And lonely her bridegroom's soul hath flown,*
            Little brother."
        (O Mother, Mary Mother,
The lonely ghost, between Hell and Heaven!)

SISTER HELEN

" Oh the wind is sad in the iron chill,
Sister Helen,
And weary sad they look by the hill."
" But he and I are sadder still,
Little brother ! "
(O Mother, Mary Mother,
Most sad of all, between Hell and Heaven !)

" See, see, the wax has dropped from its place,
Sister Helen,
And the flames are winning up apace ! "
" Yet here they burn but for a space,
Little brother ! "
(O Mother, Mary Mother,
Here for a space, between Hell and Heaven !)

" Ah ! what white thing at the door has cross'd,
Sister Helen ?
Ah ! what is this that sighs in the frost ? "
" A soul that's lost as mine is lost,
Little brother ! "
(O Mother, Mary Mother,
Lost, lost, all lost, between Hell and Heaven !)

CHIMES.

I.

H ONEY-FLOWERS *to the honey-comb*
And the honey-bee's from home.

A honey-comb and a honey-flower,
And the bee shall have his hour.

A honeyed heart for the honey-comb,
And the humming bee flies home.

A heavy heart in the honey-flower,
And the bee has had his hour.

II.

A honey cell's in the honeysuckle,
And the honey-bee knows it well.

The honey-comb has a heart of honey,
And the humming bee's so bonny.

A honey-flower's the honeysuckle,
And the bee's in the honey-bell.

The honeysuckle is sucked of honey,
And the bee is heavy and bonny.

CHIMES

III.

Brown shell first for the butterfly
And a bright wing by and by.

Butterfly, good-bye to your shell,
And, bright wings, speed you well.

'Bright lamplight for the butterfly
And a burnt wing by and by.

Butterfly, alas for your shell,
And, bright wings, fare you well.

IV.

Lost love-labour and lullaby,
And lowly let love lie.

Lost love-morrow and love-fellow
And love's life lying low.

Lovelorn labour and life laid by
And lowly let love lie.

Late love-longing and life-sorrow
And love's life lying low.

V.

Beauty's body and benison
With a bosom-flower new blown.

'Bitter beauty and blessing bann'd
With a breast to burn and brand.

Beauty's bower in the dust o'erblown
With a bare white breast of bone.

Barren beauty and bower of sand
With a blast on either hand.

CHIMES

VI.

'Buried bars in the breakwater
And bubble of the brimming weir.

'Body's blood in the breakwater
And a buried body's bier.

Buried bones in the breakwater
And bubble of the brawling weir.

'Bitter tears in the breakwater
And a breaking heart to bear.

VII.

Hollow heaven and the hurricane
And hurry of the heavy rain.

Hurried clouds in the hollow heaven
And a heavy rain hard-driven.

The heavy rain it hurries amain
And heaven and the hurricane.

Hurrying wind o'er the heaven's hollow
And the heavy rain to follow.

SOOTHSAY.

L ET *no man ask thee of anything*
Not yearborn between Spring and Spring.
More of all worlds than he can know,
Each day the single sun doth show.
A trustier gloss than thou canst give
From all wise scrolls demonstrative,
The sea doth sigh and the wind sing.

Let no man awe thee on any height
Of earthly kingship's mouldering might.
The dust his heel holds meet for thy brow
Hath all of it been what both are now;
And thou and he may plague together
A beggar's eyes in some dusty weather
When none that is now knows sound or sight.

Crave thou no dower of earthly things
Unworthy Hope's imaginings.
To have brought true birth of Song to be
And to have won hearts to Poesy,
Or anywhere in the sun or rain
To have loved and been beloved again,
Is loftiest reach of Hope's bright wings.

The wild waifs cast up by the sea
Are diverse ever seasonably.
Even so the soul-tides still may land
A different drift upon the sand.
But one the sea is evermore:
And one be still, 'twixt shore and shore,
As the sea's life, thy soul in thee.

SOOTHSAY

Say, hast thou pride?   How then may fit
Thy mood with flatterers' silk-spun wit?
Haply the sweet voice lifts thy crest,
A breeze of fame made manifest.
Nay, but then chaf'st at flattery?   Pause:
Be sure thy wrath is not because
It makes thee feel thou lovest it.

Let thy soul strive that still the same
Be early friendship's sacred flame.
The affinities have strongest part
In youth, and draw men heart to heart:
As life wears on and finds no rest,
The individual in each breast
Is tyrannous to sunder them.

In the life-drama's stern cue-call,
A friend's a part well-prized by all:
And if thou meet an enemy
What art thou that none such should be?
Even so: but if the two parts run
Into each other and grow one,
Then comes the curtain's cue to fall.

Whate'er by other's need is claimed
More than by thine, — to him unblamed
Resign it: and if he should hold
What more than he thou lack'st, bread, gold,
Or any good whereby we live, —
To thee such substance let him give
Freely: nor he nor thou be shamed.

Strive that thy works prove equal: lest
That work which thou hast done the best
Should come to be to thee at length
(Even as to envy seems the strength
Of others) hateful and abhorr'd, —
Thine own above thyself made lord, —
Of self-rebuke the bitterest.

SOOTHSAY

Unto the man of yearning thought
And aspiration, to do nought
Is in itself almost an act, —
Being chasm-fire and cataract
Of the soul's utter depths unseal'd.
Yet woe to thee if once thou yield
Unto the act of doing nought!

How callous seems beyond revoke
The clock with its last listless stroke!
How much too late at length! — to trace
The hour on its forewarning face,
The thing thou hast not dared to do! . . .
Behold, this may be thus! Ere true
It prove, arise and bear thy yoke.

Let lore of all Theology
Be to thy soul what it can *be:*
But know, — the Power that fashions man
Measured not out thy little span
For thee to take the meting-rod
In turn, and so approve on God
Thy science of Theometry.

To God at best, to Chance at worst,
Give thanks for good things, last as first.
But windstrown blossom is that good
Whose apple is not gratitude.
Even if no prayer uplift thy face,
Let the sweet right to render grace
As thy soul's cherished child be nurs'd.

Didst ever say, " Lo, I forget" ?
Such thought was to remember yet.
As in a gravegarth, count to see
The monuments of memory.
Be this thy soul's appointed scope : —
Gaze onward without claim to hope,
Nor, gazing backward, court regret.

A LITTLE WHILE.

A LITTLE *while a little love*
  The hour yet bears for thee and me
  Who have not drawn the veil to see
If still our heaven be lit above.
Thou merely, at the day's last sigh,
  Hast felt thy soul prolong the tone;
And I have heard the night-wind cry
  And deemed its speech mine own.

A little while a little love
  The scattering autumn hoards for us
  Whose bower is not yet ruinous
Nor quite unleaved our songless grove.
Only across the shaken boughs
  We hear the flood-tides seek the sea,
And deep in both our hearts they rouse
  One wail for thee and me.

A little while a little love
  May yet be ours who have not said
  The word it makes our eyes afraid
To know that each is thinking of.
Not yet the end: be our lips dumb
  In smiles a little season yet:
I'll tell thee, when the end is come,
  How we may best forget.

LOVE'S NOCTURN.

MASTER *of the murmuring courts*
   Where the shapes of sleep convene!—
Lo! my spirit here exhorts
   All the powers of thy demesne
   For their aid to woo my queen.
         What reports
   Yield thy jealous courts unseen?

Vaporous, unaccountable,
   Dreamworld lies forlorn of light,
Hollow like a breathing shell.
   Ah! that from all dreams I might
   Choose one dream and guide its flight!
         I know well
   What her sleep should tell to-night.

There the dreams are multitudes:
   Some that will not wait for sleep,
Deep within the August woods;
   Some that hum while rest may steep
   Weary labour laid a-heap;
         Interludes,
   Some, of grievous moods that weep.

'Poets' fancies all are there:
   There the elf-girls flood with wings
Valleys full of plaintive air;
   There breathe perfumes; there in rings
   Whirl the foam-bewildered springs;
         Siren there
   Winds her dizzy hair and sings.

LOVE'S NOCTURN

Thence the one dream mutually
Dreamed in bridal unison,
Less than waking ecstasy;
Half-formed visions that make moan
In the house of birth alone;
And what we
At death's wicket see, unknown.

But for mine own sleep, it lies
In one gracious form's control,
Fair with honourable eyes,
Lamps of a translucent soul:
O their glance is loftiest dole,
Sweet and wise,
Wherein Love descries his goal.

Reft of her, my dreams are all
Clammy trance that fears the sky:
Changing footpaths shift and fall;
From polluted coverts nigh,
Miserable phantoms sigh;
Quakes the pall,
And the funeral goes by.

Master, is it soothly said
That, as echoes of man's speech
Far in secret clefts are made,
So do all men's bodies reach
Shadows o'er thy sunken beach,—
Shape or shade
In those halls pourtrayed of each?

Ah! might I, by thy good grace
Groping in the windy stair,
(Darkness and the breath of space
Like loud waters everywhere,)
Meeting mine own image there
Face to face,
Send it from that place to her!

50

LOVE'S NOCTURN

Nay, not I; but oh! do thou,
  Master, from thy shadow kind
Call my body's phantom now :
  'Bid it bear its face declin'd
  Till its flight her slumbers find,
    And her brow
  Feel its presence bow like wind.

Where in groves the gracile Spring
  Trembles, with mute orison
Confidently strengthening,
  Water's voice and wind's as one
  Shed an echo in the sun.
      Soft as Spring,
  Master, bid it sing and moan.

Song shall tell how glad and strong
  Is the night she soothes alway ;
Moan shall grieve with that parched tongue
  Of the brazen hours of day :
  Sounds as of the springtide they,
      Moan and song,
  While the chill months long for May.

Not the prayers which with all leave
  The world's fluent woes prefer,—
Not the praise the world doth give,
  'Dulcet fulsome whisperer ;—
  Let it yield my love to her,
      And achieve
  Strength that shall not grieve or err.

Wheresoe'er my dreams befall,
  Both at night-watch, (let it say,)
And where round the sundial
  The reluctant hours of day,
  Heartless, hopeless of their way,
      Rest and call ;—
  There her glance doth fall and stay.

LOVE'S NOCTURN

Suddenly her face is there:
  So do mounting vapours wreathe
Subtle-scented transports where
    The black firwood sets its teeth
    Part the boughs and look beneath,—
        Lilies share
    Secret waters there, and breathe.

Master, bid my shadow bend
    Whispering thus till birth of light,
Lest new shapes that sleep may send
    Scatter all its work to flight;—
    Master, master of the night,
        Bid it spend
    Speech, song, prayer, and end aright.

Yet, ah me! if at her head
    There another phantom lean
Murmuring o'er the fragrant bed,—
    Ah! and if my spirit's queen
    Smile those alien prayers between,—
        Ah! poor shade!
    Shall it strive, or fade unseen?

How should love's own messenger
    Strive with love and be love's foe?
Master, nay! If thus, in her,
    Sleep a wedded heart should show,—
    Silent let mine image go,
        Its old share
    Of thy spell-bound air to know.

Like a vapour wan and mute,
    Like a flame, so let it pass;
One low sigh across her lute,
    One dull breath against her glass;
    And to my sad soul, alas!
        One salute
    Cold as when death's foot shall pass.

52

LOVE'S NOCTURN

Then, too, let all hopes of mine,
All vain hopes by night and day,
Slowly at thy summoning sign
Rise up pallid and obey.
Dreams, if this is thus, were they : —
Be they thine,
And to dreamworld pine away.

Yet from old time, life, not death,
Master, in thy rule is rife :
Lo! through thee, with mingling breath,
Adam woke beside his wife.
O Love bring me so, for strife,
Force and faith,
Bring me so not death but life!

Yea, to Love himself is pour'd
This frail song of hope and fear.
Thou art Love, of one accord
With kind Sleep to bring her near,
Still-eyed, deep-eyed, ah how dear!
Master, Lord,
In her name implor'd, O hear!

TROY TOWN.

Heavenborn Helen, *Sparta's queen*,
     (O Troy Town!)
Had two breasts of heavenly sheen,
The sun and moon of the heart's desire:
All Love's lordship lay between.
     (O Troy's down,
      Tall Troy's on fire!)

Helen knelt at Venus' shrine,
     (O Troy Town!)
Saying, " A little gift is mine,
A little gift for a heart's desire.
Hear me speak and make me a sign!
     (O Troy's down,
      Tall Troy's on fire!)

" Look, I bring thee a carven cup;
     (O Troy Town!)
See it here as I hold it up,—
Shaped it is to the heart's desire,
Fit to fill when the gods would sup.
     (O Troy's down,
      Tall Troy's on fire!)

" It was moulded like my breast;
     (O Troy Town!)
He that sees it may not rest,
Rest at all for his heart's desire.
O give ear to my heart's behest!
     (O Troy's down,
      Tall Troy's on fire!)

TROY TOWN

"See my breast, how like it is;
            (O Troy Town!)
See it bare for the air to kiss!
Is the cup to thy heart's desire?
O for the breast, O make it his!
            (O Troy's down,
               Tall Troy's on fire!)

" Yea, for my bosom here I sue;
            (O Troy Town!)
Thou must give it where 'tis due,
Give it there to the heart's desire.
Whom do I give my bosom to?
            (O Troy's down,
               Tall Troy's on fire!)

" Each twin breast is an apple sweet.
            (O Troy Town!)
Once an apple stirred the beat
Of thy heart with the heart's desire: —
Say, who brought it then to thy feet?
            (O Troy's down,
               Tall Troy's on fire!)

" They that claimed it then were three:
            (O Troy Town!)
For thy sake two hearts did he
Make forlorn of the heart's desire.
Do for him as he did for thee!
            (O Troy's down,
               Tall Troy's on fire!)

" Mine are apples grown to the south,
            (O Troy Town!)
Grown to taste in the days of drouth,
Taste and waste to the heart's desire:
Mine are apples meet for his mouth."
            (O Troy's down,
               Tall Troy's on fire!)

55

TROY TOWN

Venus looked on Helen's gift,
      (O Troy Town!)
Looked and smiled with subtle drift,
Saw the work of her heart's desire:—
" There thou kneel'st for Love to lift!"
      (O Troy's down,
      Tall Troy's on fire!)

Venus looked in Helen's face,
      (O Troy Town!)
Knew far off an hour and place,
And fire lit from the heart's desire;
Laughed and said, " Thy gift hath grace!"
      (O Troy's down,
      Tall Troy's on fire!)

Cupid looked on Helen's breast,
      (O Troy Town!)
Saw the heart within its nest,
Saw the flame of the heart's desire,—
Marked his arrow's burning crest.
      (O Troy's down,
      Tall Troy's on fire!)

Cupid took another dart,
      (O Troy Town!)
Fledged it for another heart,
Winged the shaft with the heart's desire,
Drew the string and said, " Depart!"
      (O Troy's down,
      Tall Troy's on fire!)

Paris turned upon his bed,
      (O Troy Town!)
Turned upon his bed and said,
Dead at heart with the heart's desire,—
" Oh to clasp her golden head!"
      (O Troy's down,
      Tall Troy's on fire!)

THE BURDEN OF NINEVEH.

In our Museum galleries
 To-day I lingered o'er the prize
Dead Greece vouchsafes to living eyes,—
Her Art for ever in fresh wise
 From hour to hour rejoicing me.
Sighing I turned at last to win
Once more the London dirt and din;
And as I made the swing-door spin
And issued, they were hoisting in
 A wingèd beast from Nineveh.

A human face the creature wore,
And hoofs behind and hoofs before,
And flanks with dark runes fretted o'er
'Twas bull, 'twas mitred Minotaur,
 A dead disbowelled mystery:
The mummy of a buried faith
Stark from the charnel without scathe,
Its wings stood for the light to bathe,—
Such fossil cerements as might swathe
 The very corpse of Nineveh.

The print of its first rush-wrapping,
Wound ere it dried, still ribbed the thing.
What song did the brown maidens sing,
From purple mouths alternating,
 When that was woven languidly?
What vows, what rites, what prayers preferr'd,
What songs has the strange image heard?
In what blind vigil stood interr'd
For ages, till an English word
 Broke silence first at Nineveh?

THE BURDEN OF NINEVEH

Oh when upon each sculptured court,
Where even the wind might not resort, —
O'er which Time passed, of like import
With the wild Arab boys at sport, —
  A living face looked in to see : —
Oh seemed it not — the spell once broke —
As though the carven warriors woke,
As though the shaft the string forsook,
The cymbals clashed, the chariots shook,
  And there was life in Nineveh?

On London stones our sun anew
The beast's recovered shadow threw.
(No shade that plague of darkness knew,
No light, no shade, while older grew
  By ages the old earth and sea.)
Lo thou! could all thy priests have shown
Such proof to make thy godhead known?
From their dead Past thou liv'st alone ;
And still thy shadow is thine own,
  Even as of yore in Nineveh.

That day whereof we keep record,
When near thy city-gates the Lord
Sheltered His Jonah with a gourd,
This sun, (I said) here present, pour'd
  Even thus this shadow that I see.
This shadow has been shed the same
From sun and moon, — from lamps which came
For prayer, — from fifteen days of flame,
The last, while smouldered to a name
  Sardanapalus' Nineveh.

Within thy shadow, haply, once
Sennacherib has knelt, whose sons
Smote him between the altar-stones :
Or pale Semiramis her zones
  Of gold, her incense brought to thee,
In love for grace, in war for aid: . . . .

THE BURDEN OF NINEVEH

Ay, and who else ? . . . . till 'neath thy shade
Within his trenches newly made
Last year the Christian knelt and pray'd—
Not to thy strength—in Nineveh.*

Now, thou poor god, within this hall
Where the blank windows blind the wall
From pedestal to pedestal,
The kind of light shall on thee fall
  Which London takes the day to be:
While school-foundations in the act
Of holiday, three files compact,
Shall learn to view thee as a fact
Connected with that zealous tract:
  "Rome,—Babylon and Nineveh."

Deemed they of this, those worshippers,
When, in some mythic chain of verse
Which man shall not again rehearse,
The faces of thy ministers
  Yearned pale with bitter ecstasy?
Greece, Egypt, Rome,—did any god
Before whose feet men knelt unshod
Deem that in this unblest abode
Another scarce more unknown god
  Should house with him, from Nineveh?

Ah! in what quarries lay the stone
From which this pillared pile has grown,
Unto man's need how long unknown,
Since those thy temples, court and cone,
  Rose far in desert history?
Ah! what is here that does not lie
All strange to thine awakened eye?
Ah! what is here can testify
(Save that dumb presence of the sky)
  Unto thy day and Nineveh?

---

* During the excavations, the Tiyari workmen held
their services in the shadow of the great bulls.—(Layard's
"Nineveh," ch. ix.)

THE BURDEN OF NINEVEH

Why, of those mummies in the room
Above, there might indeed have come
One out of Egypt to thy home,
An alien. Nay, but were not some
*   Of these thine own " antiquity " ?*
And now,—they and their gods and thou
All relics here together,—now
Whose profit ? whether bull or cow,
Isis or Ibis, who or how,
*   Whether of Thebes or Nineveh ?*

The consecrated metals found,
And ivory tablets, underground,
Winged teraphim and creatures crown'd,
When air and daylight filled the mound,
*   Fell into dust immediately.*
And even as these, the images
Of awe and worship,—even as these,—
So, smitten with the sun's increase,
Her glory mouldered and did cease
*   From immemorial Nineveh.*

The day her builders made their halt,
Those cities of the lake of salt
Stood firmly 'stablished without fault,
Made proud with pillars of basalt,
*   With sardonyx and porphyry.*
The day that Jonah bore abroad
To Nineveh the voice of God,
A brackish lake lay in his road,
Where erst Pride fixed her sure abode,
*   As then in royal Nineveh.*

The day when he, Pride's lord and Man's,
Showed all the kingdoms at a glance
To Him before whose countenance
The years recede, the years advance,
*   And said, Fall down and worship me :—*
'Mid all the pomp beneath that look,

THE BURDEN OF NINEVEH

Then stirred there, haply, some rebuke,
Where to the wind the Salt Pools shook,
And in those tracts, of life forsook,
  That knew thee not, O Nineveh!

Delicate harlot! On thy throne
Thou with a world beneath thee prone
In state for ages sat'st alone ;
And needs were years and lustres flown
  Ere strength of man could vanquish thee :
Whom even thy victor foes must bring,
Still royal, among maids that sing
As with doves' voices, taboring
Upon their breasts, unto the King,—
  A kingly conquest, Nineveh!

. . . Here woke my thought. The wind's slow sway
Had waxed ; and like the human play
Of scorn that smiling spreads away,
The sunshine shivered off the day :
  The callous wind, it seemed to me,
Swept up the shadow from the ground :
And pale as whom the Fates astound,
The god forlorn stood winged and crown'd :
Within I knew the cry lay bound
  Of the dumb soul of Nineveh.

And as I turned, my sense half shut
Still saw the crowds of kerb and rut
Go past as marshalled to the strut
Of ranks in gypsum quaintly cut.
  It seemed in one same pageantry
They followed forms which had been erst ;
To pass, till on my sight should burst
That future of the best or worst
When some may question which was first,
  Of London or of Nineveh.

THE BURDEN OF NINEVEH

*For as that Bull-god once did stand
And watched the burial-clouds of sand,
Till these at last without a hand
Rose o'er his eyes, another land,
   And blinded him with destiny : —
So may he stand again; till now,
In ships of unknown sail and prow,
Some tribe of the Australian plough
Bear him afar, — a relic now
   Of London, not of Nineveh!*

*Or it may chance indeed that when
Man's age is hoary among men, —
His centuries threescore and ten, —
His furthest childhood shall seem then
   More clear than later times may be:
Who, finding in this desert place
This form, shall hold us for some race
That walked not in Christ's lowly ways,
But bowed its pride and vowed its praise
   Unto the God of Nineveh.*

*The smile rose first, — anon drew nigh
The thought : . . Those heavy wings spread high,
So sure of flight, which do not fly;
That set gaze never on the sky;
   Those scriptured flanks it cannot see;
Its crown, a brow-contracting load;
Its planted feet which trust the sod : . . .
(So grew the image as I trod :)
O Nineveh, was this thy God, —
   Thine also, mighty Nineveh?*

THE SONG OF THE BOWER.

Say, *is it day, is it dusk in thy bower,*
  Thou whom I long for, who longest for me?
Oh! be it light, be it night, 'tis Love's hour,
  Love's that is fettered as Love's that is free.
Free Love has leaped to that innermost chamber,
  Oh! the last time, and the hundred before:
Fettered Love, motionless, can but remember,
  Yet something that sighs from him passes the door.

Nay, but my heart when it flies to thy bower,
  What does it find there that knows it again?
There it must droop like a shower-beaten flower,
  Red at the rent core and dark with the rain.
Ah! yet what shelter is still shed above it,—
  What waters still image its leaves torn apart?
Thy soul is the shade that clings round it to love it,
  And tears are its mirror deep down in thy heart.

What were my prize, could I enter thy bower,
  This day, to-morrow, at eve or at morn?
Large lovely arms and a neck like a tower,
  Bosom then heaving that now lies forlorn.
Kindled with love-breath, (the sun's kiss is colder!)
  Thy sweetness all near me, so distant to-day;
My hand round thy neck and thy hand on my shoulder,
  My mouth to thy mouth as the world melts away.

What is it keeps me afar from thy bower,—
  My spirit, my body, so fain to be there?
Waters engulfing or fires that devour?—
  Earth heaped against me or death in the air?

THE SONG OF THE BOWER

Nay, but in day-dreams, for terror, for pity,
  The trees wave their heads with an omen to tell;
Nay, but in night-dreams, throughout the dark city,
  The hours, clashed together, lose count in the bell.

Shall I not one day remember thy bower,
  One day when all days are one day to me? —
Thinking, " I stirred not, and yet had the power!" —
  Yearning, " Ah God, if again it might be!"
Peace, peace! such a small lamp illumes, on this highway,
  So dimly so few steps in front of my feet, —
Yet shows me that her way is parted from my way. . . .
  Out of sight, beyond light, at what goal may we meet?

JENNY.

Vengeance of Jenny's case! Fie on her! Never name her, child!

(MRS. QUICKLY.)

L AZY *laughing languid Jenny,*
 Fond of a kiss and fond of a guinea,
Whose head upon my knee to-night
Rests for a while, as if grown light
With all our dances and the sound
To which the wild tunes spun you round:
Fair Jenny mine, the thoughtless queen
Of kisses which the blush between
Could hardly make much daintier;
Whose eyes are as blue skies, whose hair
Is countless gold incomparable:
Fresh flower, scarce touched with signs that tell
Of Love's exuberant hotbed:—Nay,
Poor flower left torn since yesterday
Until to-morrow leave you bare;
Poor handful of bright spring-water
Flung in the whirlpool's shrieking face;
Poor shameful Jenny, full of grace
Thus with your head upon my knee;—
Whose person or whose purse may be
The lodestar of your reverie?

This room of yours, my Jenny, looks
A change from mine so full of books,
Whose serried ranks hold fast, forsooth,
So many captive hours of youth,—
The hours they thieve from day and night
To make one's cherished work come right,

JENNY

And leave it wrong for all their theft,
Even as to-night my work was left :
Until I vowed that since my brain
And eyes of dancing seemed so fain,
My feet should have some dancing too : —
And thus it was I met with you.
Well, I suppose 'twas hard to part,
For here I am.   And now, sweetheart,
You seem too tired to get to bed.

It was a careless life I led
When rooms like this were scarce so strange
Not long ago.   What breeds the change, —
The many aims or the few years ?
Because to-night it all appears
Something I do not know again.

The cloud's not danced out of my brain, —
The cloud that made it turn and swim
While hour by hour the books grew dim.
Why, Jenny, as I watch you there, —
For all your wealth of loosened hair,
Your silk ungirdled and unlac'd
And warm sweets open to the waist,
All golden in the lamplight's gleam, —
You know not what a book you seem,
Half-read by lightning in a dream!
How should you know, my Jenny ?   Nay,
And I should be ashamed to say : —
Poor beauty, so well worth a kiss!
But while my thought runs on like this
With wasteful whims more than enough,
I wonder what you're thinking of.

If of myself you think at all,
What is the thought ? — conjectural

JENNY

On sorry matters best unsolved? —
Or inly is each grace revolved
To fit me with a lure? — or (sad
To think!) perhaps you're merely glad
That I'm not drunk or ruffianly
And let you rest upon my knee.

For sometimes, were the truth confess'd,
You're thankful for a little rest, —
Glad from the crush to rest within,
From the heart-sickness and the din
Where envy's voice at virtue's pitch
Mocks you because your gown is rich;
And from the pale girl's dumb rebuke,
Whose ill-clad grace and toil-worn look
Proclaim the strength that keeps her weak
And other nights than yours bespeak;
And from the wise unchildish elf,
To schoolmate lesser than himself,
Pointing you out, what thing you are: —
Yes, from the daily jeer and jar,
From shame and shame's outbraving too,
Is rest not sometimes sweet to you? —
But most from the hatefulness of man
Who spares not to end what he began,
Whose acts are ill and his speech ill,
Who, having used you at his will,
Thrusts you aside, as when I dine
I serve the dishes and the wine.

Well, handsome Jenny mine, sit up,
I've filled our glasses, let us sup,
And do not let me think of you,
Lest shame of yours suffice for two.
What, still so tired? Well, well then, keep
Your head there, so you do not sleep;
But that the weariness may pass

67

JENNY

And leave you merry, take this glass.
Ah! lazy lily hand, more bless'd
If ne'er in rings it had been dress'd
Nor ever by a glove conceal'd!

Behold the lilies of the field,
They toil not neither do they spin;
(So doth the ancient text begin,—
Not of such rest as one of these
Can share.) Another rest and ease
Along each summer-sated path
From its new lord the garden hath,
Than that whose spring in blessings ran
Which praised the bounteous husbandman,
Ere yet, in days of hankering breath,
The lilies sickened unto death.

What, Jenny, are your lilies dead?
Aye, and the snow-white leaves are spread
Like winter on the garden-bed.
But you had roses left in May,—
They were not gone too. Jenny, nay,
But must your roses die, and those
Their purfled buds that should unclose?
Even so; the leaves are curled apart,
Still red as from the broken heart,
And here's the naked stem of thorns.

Nay, nay, mere words. Here nothing warns
As yet of winter. Sickness here
Or want alone could waken fear,—
Nothing but passion wrings a tear.
Except when there may rise unsought
Haply at times a passing thought
Of the old days which seem to be
Much older than any history
That is written in any book;
When she would lie in fields and look

JENNY

Along the ground through the blown grass,
And wonder where the city was,
Far out of sight, whose broil and bale
They told her then for a child's tale.

Jenny, you know the city now.
A child can tell the tale there, how
Some things which are not yet enroll'd
In market-lists are bought and sold
Even till the early Sunday light,
When Saturday night is market-night
Everywhere, be it dry or wet,
And market-night in the Haymarket.
Our learned London children know,
Poor Jenny, all your pride and woe;
Have seen your lifted silken skirt
Advertise dainties through the dirt;
Have seen your coach-wheels splash rebuke
On virtue; and have learned your look
When, wealth and health slipped past, you stare
Along the streets alone, and there,
Round the long park, across the bridge,
The cold lamps at the pavement's edge
Wind on together and apart,
A fiery serpent for your heart.

Let the thoughts pass, an empty cloud!
Suppose I were to think aloud,—
What if to her all this were said?
Why, as a volume seldom read
Being opened halfway shuts again,
So might the pages of her brain
Be parted at such words, and thence
Close back upon the dusty sense.
For is there hue or shape defin'd
In Jenny's desecrated mind,
Where all contagious currents meet,
A Lethe of the middle street?

JENNY

Nay, it reflects not any face,
Nor sound is in its sluggish pace,
But as they coil those eddies clot,
And night and day remember not.

Why, Jenny, you're asleep at last! —
Asleep, poor Jenny, hard and fast, —
So young and soft and tired; so fair,
With chin thus nestled in your hair,
Mouth quiet, eyelids almost blue
As if some sky of dreams shone through!

Just as another woman sleeps!
Enough to throw one's thoughts in heaps
Of doubt and horror, — what to say
Or think, — this awful secret sway,
The potter's power over the clay!
Of the same lump (it has been said)
For honour and dishonour made,
Two sister vessels. Here is one.

My cousin Nell is fond of fun,
And fond of dress, and change, and praise,
So mere a woman in her ways:
And if her sweet eyes rich in youth
Are like her lips that tell the truth,
My cousin Nell is fond of love.
And she's the girl I'm proudest of.
Who does not prize her, guard her well?
The love of change, in cousin Nell,
Shall find the best and hold it dear:
The unconquered mirth turn quieter
Not through her own, through others' woe:
The conscious pride of beauty glow
Beside another's pride in her,
One little part of all they share.
For Love himself shall ripen these

JENNY

In a kind soil to just increase
Through years of fertilizing peace.

Of the same lump (as it is said)
For honour and dishonour made,
Two sister vessels.   Here is one.

It makes a goblin of the sun.

So pure, — so fall'n!   How dare to think
Of the first common kindred link?
Yet, Jenny, till the world shall burn
It seems that all things take their turn;
And who shall say but this fair tree
May need, in changes that may be,
Your children's children's charity?
Scorned then, no doubt, as you are scorn'd!
Shall no man hold his pride forewarn'd
Till in the end, the Day of Days,
At Judgment, one of his own race,
As frail and lost as you, shall rise, —
His daughter, with his mother's eyes?

How Jenny's clock ticks on the shelf!
Might not the dial scorn itself
That has such hours to register?
Yet as to me, even so to her
Are golden sun and silver moon,
In daily largesse of earth's boon,
Counted for life-coins to one tune.
And if, as blindfold fates are toss'd,
Through some one man this life be lost,
Shall soul not somehow pay for soul?

Fair shines the gilded aureole
In which our highest painters place
Some living woman's simple face.
And the stilled features thus descried

71

JENNY

As Jenny's long throat droops aside,—
The shadows where the cheeks are thin,
And pure wide curve from ear to chin,—
With Raffael's, Leonardo's hand
To show them to men's souls, might stand,
Whole ages long, the whole world through,
For preachings of what God can do.
What has man done here? How atone,
Great God, for this which man has done?
And for the body and soul which by
Man's pitiless doom must now comply
With lifelong hell, what lullaby
Of sweet forgetful second birth
Remains? All dark. No sign on earth
What measure of God's rest endows
The many mansions of his house.

If but a woman's heart might see
Such erring heart unerringly
For once! But that can never be.

Like a rose shut in a book
In which pure women may not look,
For its base pages claim control
To crush the flower within the soul;
Where through each dead rose-leaf that clings,
Pale as transparent Psyche-wings,
To the vile text, are traced such things
As might make lady's cheek indeed
More than a living rose to read;
So nought save foolish foulness may
Watch with hard eyes the sure decay;
And so the life-blood of this rose,
Puddled with shameful knowledge, flows
Through leaves no chaste hand may unclose;
Yet still it keeps such faded show
Of when 'twas gathered long ago,
That the crushed petals' lovely grain,

JENNY

The sweetness of the sanguine stain,
Seen of a woman's eyes, must make
Her pitiful heart, so prone to ache,
Love roses better for its sake : —
Only that this can never be : —
Even so unto her sex is she.

Yet, Jenny, looking long at you,
The woman almost fades from view.
A cipher of man's changeless sum
Of lust, past, present, and to come,
Is left. A riddle that one shrinks
To challenge from the scornful sphinx.

Like a toad within a stone
Seated while Time crumbles on ;
Which sits there since the earth was curs'd
For Man's transgression at the first ;
Which, living through all centuries,
Not once has seen the sun arise ;
Whose life, to its cold circle charmed,
The earth's whole summers have not warmed ;
Which always — whitherso the stone
Be flung — sits there, deaf, blind, alone ; —
Aye, and shall not be driven out
Till that which shuts him round about
Break at the very Master's stroke,
And the dust thereof vanish as smoke,
And the seed of Man vanish as dust : —
Even so within this world is Lust.

Come, come, what use in thoughts like this ?
Poor little Jenny, good to kiss, —
You'd not believe by what strange roads
Thought travels, when your beauty goads
A man to-night to think of toads !
enny, wake up. . . . Why, there's the dawn !

JENNY

*And there's an early waggon drawn
To market, and some sheep that jog
Bleating before a barking dog;
And the old streets come peering through
Another night that London knew;
And all as ghostlike as the lamps.*

*So on the wings of day decamps
My last night's frolic. Glooms begin
To shiver off as lights creep in
Past the gauze curtains half drawn-to,
And the lamp's doubled shade grows blue,—
Your lamp, my Jenny, kept alight,
Like a wise virgin's, all one night!
And in the alcove coolly spread
Glimmers with dawn your empty bed;
And yonder your fair face I see
Reflected lying on my knee,
Where teems with first foreshadowings
Your pier-glass scrawled with diamond rings:
And on your bosom all night worn
Yesterday's rose now droops forlorn
But dies not yet this summer morn.*

*And now without, as if some word
Had called upon them that they heard,
The London sparrows far and nigh
Clamor together suddenly;
And Jenny's cage-bird grown awake
Here in their song his part must take,
Because here too the day doth break.*

*And somehow in myself the dawn
Among stirred clouds and veils withdrawn
Strikes greyly on her. Let her sleep.
But will it wake her if I heap
These cushions thus beneath her head
Where my knee was? No,—there's your bed,*

74

JENNY

My Jenny, while you dream.   And there
I lay among your golden hair
Perhaps the subject of your dreams,
These golden coins.
                            For still one deems
That Jenny's flattering sleep confers
New magic on the magic purse, —
Grim web, how clogged with shrivelled flies!
Between the threads fine fumes arise
And shape their pictures in the brain.
There roll no streets in glare and rain,
Nor flagrant man-swine whets his tusk;
But delicately sighs in musk
The homage of the dim boudoir;
Or like a palpitating star
Thrilled into song, the opera-night
Breathes faint in the quick pulse of light;
Or at the carriage-window shine
Rich wares for choice; or, free to dine,
Whirls through its hour of health (divine
For her) the concourse of the Park.
And though in the discounted dark
Her functions there and here are one,
Beneath the lamps and in the sun
There reigns at least the acknowledged belle
Apparelled beyond parallel.
Ah, Jenny, yes, we know your dreams.

For even the Paphian Venus seems
A goddess o'er the realms of love,
When silver-shrined in shadowy grove:
Aye, or let offerings nicely placed
But hide Priapus to the waist,
And whoso looks on him shall see
An eligible deity.

Why, Jenny, waking here alone
May help you to remember one,

JENNY

Though all the memory's long outworn
Of many a double-pillowed morn.
I think I see you when you wake,
And rub your eyes for me, and shake
My gold, in rising, from your hair,
A Danaë for a moment there.

Jenny, my love rang true! for still
Love at first sight is vague, until
That tinkling makes him audible.

And must I mock you to the last,
Ashamed of my own shame, — aghast
Because some thoughts not born amiss
Rose at a poor fair face like this?
Well, of such thoughts so much I know:
In my life, as in hers, they show,
By a far gleam which I may near,
A dark path I can strive to clear.

Only one kiss. Good-bye, my dear.

STRATTON WATER.

" O HAVE you seen the Stratton flood
    That's great with rain to-day?
It runs beneath your wall, Lord Sands,
    Full of the new-mown hay.

"I led your hounds to Hutton bank
    To bathe at early morn:
They got their bath by Borrowbrake
    Above the standing corn."

Out from the castle-stair Lord Sands
    Looked up the western lea;
The rook was grieving on her nest,
    The flood was round her tree.

Over the castle-wall Lord Sands
    Looked down the eastern hill:
The stakes swam free among the boats,
    The flood was rising still.

" What's yonder far below that lies
    So white against the slope?"
" O it's a sail o' your binny barks
    The waters have washed up."

"But I have never a sail so white,
    And the water's not yet there."
" O it's the swans o' your bonny lake
    The rising flood doth scare."

STRATTON WATER

" *The swans they would not hold so still,*
  So high they would not win."
" *O it's Joyce my wife has spread her smock*
  And fears to fetch it in."

" *Nay, knave, it's neither sail nor swans,*
  Nor aught that you can say;
For though your wife might leave her smock,
  Herself she'd bring away."

Lord Sands has passed the turret-stair,
  The court, and yard, and all;
The kine were in the byre that day,
  The nags were in the stall.

Lord Sands has won the weltering slope
  Whereon the white shape lay:
The clouds were still above the hill,
  And the shape was still as they.

Oh pleasant is the gaze of life
  And sad is death's blind head;
But awful are the living eyes
  In the face of one thought dead!

" *In God's name, Janet, is it me*
  Thy ghost has come to seek?"
" *Nay, wait another hour, Lord Sands, —*
  Be sure my ghost shall speak."

A moment stood he as a stone,
  Then grovelled to his knee.
" *O Janet, O my love, my love,*
  Rise up and come with me!"
" *O once before you bade me come,*
  And it's here you have brought me!

78

STRATTON WATER

" *O many's the sweet word, Lord Sands,*
  You've spoken oft to me ;
But all that I have from you to-day
  Is the rain on my body.

" *And many's the good gift, Lord Sands,*
  You've promised oft to me ;
But the gift of yours I keep to-day
  Is the babe in my body.

" *O it's not in any earthly bed*
  That first my babe I'll see ;
For I have brought my body here
  That the flood may cover me."

His face was close against her face,
  His hands of hers were fain :
O her wet cheeks were hot with tears,
  Her wet hands cold with rain.

" *They told me you were dead, Janet, —*
  How could I guess the lie ?"
" *They told me you were false, Lord Sands, —*
  What could I do but die ?"

" *Now keep you well, my brother Giles, —*
  Through you I deemed her dead !
As wan as your towers be to-day,
  To-morrow they'll be red.

" *Look down, look down, my false mother,*
  That bade me not to grieve :
You'll look up when our marriage fires
  Are lit to-morrow eve.

79

STRATTON WATER

" O more than one and more than two
The sorrow of this shall see :
But it's to-morrow, love, for them, —
To-day's for thee and me."

He's drawn her face between his hands
And her pale mouth to his :
No bird that was so still that day
Chirps sweeter than his kiss.

The flood was creeping round their feet.
" O Janet, come away !
The hall is warm for the marriage-rite,
The bed for the birthday."

" Nay, but I hear your mother cry,
' Go bring this bride to bed !
And would she christen her babe unborn,
So wet she comes to wed ? '

" I'll be your wife to cross your door
And meet your mother's e'e.
We plighted troth to wed i' the kirk,
And it's there you'll wed with me."

He's ta'en her by the short girdle
And by the dripping sleeve :
" Go fetch Sir Jock my mother's priest, —
You'll ask of him no leave.

" O it's one half-hour to reach the kirk
And one for the marriage-rite ;
And kirk and castle and castle-lands
Shall be our babe's to-night."

STRATTON WATER

" *The flood's in the kirkyard, Lord Sands,*
  And round the belfry-stair."
" *I bade you fetch the priest,*" *he said,*
  " *Myself shall bring him there.*

" *It's for the lilt of wedding bells*
  We'll have the hail to pour,
And for the clink of bridle-reins
  The plashing of the oar."

Beneath them on the nether hill
  A boat was floating wide:
Lord Sands swam out and caught the oars
  And rowed to the hill-side.

He's wrapped her in a green mantle
  And set her softly in;
Her hair was wet upon her face,
  Her face was grey and thin;
And " Oh!" she said, " lie still, my babe,
  It's out you must not win!"

But woe's my heart for Father John
  As hard as he might pray,
There seemed no help but Noah's ark
  Or Jonah's fish that day.

The first strokes that the oars struck
  Were over the broad leas;
The next strokes that the oars struck
  They pushed beneath the trees;

The last stroke that the oars struck,
  The good boat's head was met,
And there the gate of the kirkyard
  Stood like a ferry-gate.

He's set his hand upon the bar
  And lightly leaped within:

STRATTON WATER

He's lifted her to his left shoulder,
Her knees beside his chin.

The graves lay deep beneath the flood
Under the rain alone;
And when the foot-stone made him slip,
He held by the head-stone.

The empty boat thrawed i' the wind,
Against the postern tied.
"Hold still, you've brought my love with me,
You shall take back my bride."

But woe's my heart for Father John
And the saints he clamoured to!
There's never a saint but Christopher
Might hale such buttocks through!

And "Oh!" she said, "on men's shoulders
I well had thought to wend,
And well to travel with a priest,
But not to have cared or ken'd.

"And oh!" she said, "it's well this way
That I thought to have fared,—
Not to have lighted at the kirk
'But stopped in the kirkyard.

"For it's oh and oh I prayed to God,
Whose rest I hoped to win,
That when to-night at your board-head
You'd bid the feast begin,
This water past your window-sill
Might bear my body in."

Now make the white bed warm and soft
And greet the merry morn.
The night the mother should have died,
The young son shall be born.

THE STREAM'S SECRET.

W HAT *thing unto mine ear*
Wouldst thou convey,—what secret thing,
O wandering water ever whispering?
Surely thy speech shall be of her.
Thou water, O thou whispering wanderer,
What message dost thou bring?

Say, hath not Love leaned low
This hour beside thy far well-head,
And there through jealous hollowed fingers said
The thing that most I long to know,—
Murmuring with curls all dabbled in thy flow
And washed lips rosy red?

He told it to thee there
Where thy voice hath a louder tone;
But where it welters to this little moan
His will decrees that I should hear.
Now speak: for with the silence is no fear,
And I am all alone.

Shall Time not still endow
One hour with life, and I and she
Slake in one kiss the thirst of memory?
Say, stream; lest Love should disavow
Thy service, and the bird upon the bough
Sing first to tell it me.

THE STREAM'S SECRET

What whisperest thou? Nay, why
Name the dead hours? I mind them well:
Their ghosts in many darkened doorways dwell
With desolate eyes to know them by.
The hour that must be born ere it can die,—
Of that I'd have thee tell.

But hear, before thou speak!
Withhold, I pray, the vain behest
That while the maze hath still its bower for quest
My burning heart should cease to seek.
Be sure that Love ordained for souls more meek
His roadside dells of rest.

Stream, when this silver thread
In flood-time is a torrent brown
May any bulwark bind thy foaming crown?
Shall not the waters surge and spread
And to the crannied boulders of their bed
Still shoot the dead drift down?

Let no rebuke find place
In speech of thine: or it shall prove
That thou dost ill expound the words of Love,
Even as thine eddy's rippling race
Would blur the perfect image of his face.
I will have none thereof.

O learn and understand
That 'gainst the wrongs himself did wreak
Love sought her aid; until her shadowy cheek
And eyes beseeching gave command;
And compassed in her close compassionate hand
My heart must burn and speak.

THE STREAM'S SECRET

For then at last we spoke
What eyes so oft had told to eyes
Through that long-lingering silence whose half-sighs
Alone the buried secret broke,
Which with snatched hands and lips' reverberate stroke
Then from the heart did rise.

But she is far away
Now; nor the hours of night grown hoar
'Bring yet to me, long gazing from the door,
The wind-stirred robe of roseate grey
And rose-crown of the hour that leads the day
When we shall meet once more.

'Dark as thy blinded wave
When brimming midnight floods the glen,—
Bright as the laughter of thy runnels when
The dawn yields all the light they crave;
Even so these hours to wound and that to save
Are sisters in Love's ken.

Oh sweet her bending grace
Then when I kneel beside her feet;
And sweet her eyes' o'erhanging heaven; and sweet
The gathering folds of her embrace;
And her fall'n hair at last shed round my face
When breaths and tears shall meet.

'Beneath her sheltering hair,
In the warm silence near her breast,
Our kisses and our sobs shall sink to rest;
As in some still trance made aware
That day and night have wrought to fulness there
And Love has built our nest.

THE STREAM'S SECRET

And as in the dim grove,
When the rains ceased that hushed them long,
'Mid glistening boughs the song-birds wake to song, —
So from our hearts deep-shrined in love,
While the leaves throb beneath, around, above,
The quivering notes shall throng.

Till tenderest words found vain
Draw back to wonder mute and deep,
And closed lips in closed arms a silence keep,
Subdued by memory's circling strain, —
The wind-rapt sound that the wind brings again
While all the willows weep.

Then by her summoning art
Shall memory conjure back the sere
Autumnal Springs, from many a dying year
'Born dead; and, bitter to the heart,
The very ways where now we walk apart
Who then shall cling so near.

And with each thought new-grown,
Some sweet caress or some sweet name
Low-breathed shall let me know her thought the same;
Making me rich with every tone
And touch of the dear heaven so long unknown
That filled my dreams with flame.

Pity and love shall burn
In her pressed cheek and cherishing hands;
And from the living spirit of love that stands
'Between her lips to soothe and yearn,
Each separate breath shall clasp me round in turn
And loose my spirit's bands.

THE STREAM'S SECRET

Oh passing sweet and dear,
Then when the worshipped form and face
Are felt at length in darkling close embrace ;
'Round which so oft the sun shone clear,
With mocking light and pitiless atmosphere,
In many an hour and place.

Ah me ! with what proud growth
Shall that hour's thirsting race be run ;
While, for each several sweetness still begun
Afresh, endures love's endless drouth :   [mouth,
Sweet hands, sweet hair, sweet cheeks, sweet eyes, sweet
Each singly wooed and won.

Yet most with the sweet soul
Shall love's espousals then be knit ;
For very passion of peace shall breathe from it
O'er tremulous wings that touch the goal,
As on the unmeasured height of Love's control
The lustral fires are lit.

Therefore, when breast and cheek
Now part, from long embraces free, —
Each on the other gazing shall but see
A self that has no need to speak :
All things unsought, yet nothing more to seek, —
One love in unity.

O water wandering past, —
Albeit to thee I speak this thing,
O water, thou that wanderest whispering,
Thou keep'st thy counsel to the last.
What spell upon thy bosom should Love cast,
His message thence to wring ?

87

THE STREAM'S SECRET

Nay, must thou hear the tale
Of the past days,—the heavy debt
Of life that obdurate time withholds,—ere yet
To win thine ear these prayers prevail,
And by thy voice Love's self with high All-hail
Yield up the love-secret?

How should all this be told?—
All the sad sum of wayworn days;—
Heart's anguish in the impenetrable maze,
And on the waste uncoloured wold
The visible burthen of the sun grown cold
And the moon's labouring gaze?

Alas! shall hope be nurs'd
On life's all-succouring breast in vain,
And made so perfect only to be slain?
Or shall not rather the sweet thirst
Even yet rejoice the heart with warmth dispers'd
And strength grown fair again?

Stands it not by the door—
Love's Hour—till she and I shall meet
With bodiless form and unapparent feet
That cast no shadow yet before,
Though round its head the dawn begins to pour
The breath that makes day sweet?

Its eyes invisible
Watch till the dial's thin-thrown shade
Be born,—yea, till the journeying line be laid
Upon the point that wakes the spell,
And there in lovelier light than tongue can tell
Its presence stand array'd.

THE STREAM'S SECRET

Its soul remembers yet
Those sunless hours that passed it by ;
And still it hears the night's disconsolate cry,
And feels the branches wringing wet
Cast on its brow, that may not once forget,
Dumb tears from the blind sky.

But oh! when now her foot
Draws near, for whose sake night and day
Were long in weary longing sighed away,—
The Hour of Love, 'mid airs grown mute,
Shall sing beside the door, and Love's own lute
Thrill to the passionate lay.

Thou know'st, for Love has told
Within thine ear, O stream, how soon
That song shall lift its sweet appointed tune.
O tell me, for my lips are cold,
And in my veins the blood is waxing old
Even while I beg the boon.

So, in that hour of sighs
Assuaged, shall we beside this stone
Yield thanks for grace ; while in thy mirror shown
The twofold image softly lies,
Until we kiss, and each in other's eyes
Is imaged all alone.

Still silent ?   Can no art
Of Love's then move thy pity ?   Nay,
To thee let nothing come that owns his sway :
Let happy lovers have no part
With thee ; nor even so sad and poor a heart
As thou hast spurned to-day.

THE STREAM'S SECRET

To-day ? Lo ! night is here.
The glen grows heavy with some veil
Risen from the earth or fall'n to make earth pale ;
And all stands hushed to eye and ear,
Until the night-wind shake the shade like fear
And every covert quail.

Ah ! by a colder wave
On deathlier airs the hour must come
Which to thy heart, my love, shall call me home.
Between the lips of the low cave
Against that night the lapping waters lave,
And the dark lips are dumb.

But there Love's self doth stand,
And with Life's weary wings far-flown,
And with Death's eyes that make the water moan,
Gathers the water in his hand:
And they that drink know nought of sky or land
But only love alone.

O soul-sequestered face
Far off, — O were that night but now !
So even beside that stream even I and thou
Through thirsting lips should draw Love's grace,
And in the zone of that supreme embrace
Bind aching breast and brow.

O water whispering
Still through the dark into mine ears, —
As with mine eyes, is it not now with hers ? —
Mine eyes that add to thy cold spring,
Wan water, wandering water weltering,
This hidden tide of tears.

THE CARD-DEALER.

COULD *you not drink her gaze like wine ?*
Yet though its splendour swoon
Into the silence languidly
As a tune into a tune,
Those eyes unravel the coiled night
And know the stars at noon.

The gold that's heaped beside her hand,
In truth rich prize it were ;
And rich the dreams that wreathe her brows
With magic stillness there ;
And he were rich who should unwind
That woven golden hair.

Around her, where she sits, the dance
Now breathes its eager heat ;
And not more lightly or more true
Fall there the dancers' feet
Than fall her cards on the bright board
As 'twere a heart that beat.

Her fingers let them softly through,
Smooth polished silent things ;
And each one as it falls reflects
In swift light-shadowings,
Blood-red and purple, green and blue,
The great eyes of her rings.

THE CARD-DEALER

Whom plays she with ?   With thee, who lov'st
  Those gems upon her hand;
With me, who search her secret brows;
  With all men, bless'd or bann'd.
We play together, she and we,
  Within a vain strange land:

A land without any order,—
  Day even as night, (one saith,) —
Where who lieth down ariseth not
  Nor the sleeper awakeneth;
A land of darkness as darkness itself
  And of the shadow of death.

What be her cards, you ask ?   Even these: —
  The heart, that doth but crave
More, having fed; the diamond,
  Skilled to make base seem brave;
The club, for smiting in the dark;
  The spade, to dig a grave.

And do you ask what game she plays?
  With me 'tis lost or won;
With thee it is playing still; with him
  It is not well begun;
But 'tis a game she plays with all
  Beneath the sway o' the sun.

Thou seest the card that falls,— she knows
  The card that followeth:
Her game in thy tongue is called Life,
  As ebbs thy daily breath:
When she shall speak, thou'lt learn her tongue
  And know she calls it Death.

MY SISTER'S SLEEP.

SHE *fell asleep on Christmas Eve :*
At length the long ungranted shade
Of weary eyelids overweigh'd
The pain nought else might yet relieve.

Our mother, who had leaned all day
Over the bed from chime to chime,
Then raised herself for the first time,
And as she sat her down, did pray.

Her little work-table was spread
With work to finish. For the glare
Made by her candle, she had care
To work some distance from the bed.

Without, there was a cold moon up,
Of winter radiance sheer and thin;
The hollow halo it was in
Was like an icy crystal cup.

Through the small room, with subtle sound
Of flame, by vents the fireshine drove
And reddened. In its dim alcove
The mirror shed a clearness round.

I had been sitting up some nights,
And my tired mind felt weak and blank;
Like a sharp strengthening wine it drank
The stillness and the broken lights.

MY SISTER'S SLEEP

Twelve struck.   That sound, by dwindling years
  Heard in each hour, crept off; and then
  The ruffled silence spread again,
Like water that a pebble stirs.

Our mother rose from where she sat:
  Her needles, as she laid them down,
  Met lightly, and her silken gown
Settled: no other noise than that.

" Glory unto the Newly Born!"
  So, as said angels, she did say;
  Because we were in Christmas Day,
Though it would still be long till morn.

Just then in the room over us
  There was a pushing back of chairs,
  As some who had sat unawares
So late, now heard the hour, and rose.

With anxious softly-stepping haste
  Our mother went where Margaret lay,
  Fearing the sounds o'erhead — should they
Have broken her long watched-for rest!

She stopped an instant, calm, and turned;
  But suddenly turned back again;
  And all her features seemed in pain
With woe, and her eyes gazed and yearned.

For my part, I but hid my face,
  And held my breath, and spoke no word:
  There was none spoken; but I heard
The silence for a little space.

94

MY SISTER'S SLEEP

Our mother bowed herself and wept :
  And both my arms fell, and I said,
  "God knows I knew that she was dead."
And there, all white, my sister slept.

Then kneeling, upon Christmas morn
  A little after twelve o'clock
  We said, ere the first quarter struck,
"Christ's blessing on the newly born!"

Printed by CORNHILL PRESS,
Boston, Mass.
1896

CPSIA information can be obtained
at www.ICGtesting.com
Printed in the USA
LVHW111504280821
696349LV00005B/105